THOUGHT THAT NATURE

Trey Moody

WINNER OF THE 2012 KATHRYN A. MORTON PRIZE IN POETRY

SELECTED BY COLE SWENSEN

Sarabande Books

LOUISVILLE, KENTUCKY

Managing Editor
Sarabande Books, Inc.
2234 Dundee Road, Suite 200
Louisville, KY 40205

Library of Congress Cataloging-in-Publication Data

Moody, Trey, 1982–
[Poems. Selections]
Thought That Nature / Trey Moody.
    pages cm. — (The Kathryn A. Morton Prize in Poetry)
"Winner of the 2012 Kathryn A. Morton Prize in Poetry selected by Cole Swensen."
 Summary: "Like rigorous philosophy, Trey Moody's poems begin with the immediate
evidence, then move outward: "I am here," he says, "So far/this seems to have been
true." With his own existence as somewhat shaky premise, Moody is able to explore
correspondences of thought and nature, of mind and matter. His project is to identify
and capture those moments when the border between personal consciousness and
the otherness of the physical become porous: "Pin oak left/me with its leaves, each/a
somewhat familiar word." Word is just one letter away from world, and through Moody's
bemused, self-effacing explorations we begin to see just how much language shades and
even determines our day-to-day experience. Ironically, it also allows Moody to measure
the distance between consciousness and direct experience, even as he casts this gap in
memorable speech. "Wind listens," he says, "though I lack insight." This debut collection
by a poet of obvious promise offers the reader a folding together of sensual delight and
intellectual pursuit—a rare and bracing combination"—Provided by publisher.
"Winner of the 2012 Kathryn A. Morton Prize in Poetry selected by Cole Swensen."
ISBN 978-1-936747-67-2 (paperback)
I. Title.
PS3614.O549845T46 2014
811'.6—dc23

                          2013024626

Cover art: "Le Tricolore, Jeune Adulte" by René Primevère Lesson (1794–1849).

Cover and interior layout by Kirkby Gann Tittle.

Manufactured in Canada.

This book is printed on acid-free paper.

Sarabande Books is a nonprofit literary organization.

The Kentucky Arts Council, the state arts agency, supports Sarabande
Books with state tax dollars and federal funding from the National
Endowment for the Arts.

for Jennifer and Charlotte

CONTENTS

3

FOREWORD

"Everyone always talks about the weather, but no one ever does anything about it."

This classic joke has taken on an ever-more tragic twist during the past thirty years of increasingly obvious climate change, change that "we" could, should, and *must* do something about. Much international work on the issue focuses on defining that "we," which has, among other effects (none of them addressing global warming), launched an interrogation of the "we" in its many social and political aspects, with their own effects, ranging from battles over immigration policy to fiscal unions. All these issues hum subtly at the bottom of Trey Moody's sweeping collection—sweeping also in the weatherian sense; it has a tremendous momentum that amounts to a tempestuous phenomenon of wind or wave or both.

Increasingly, "weather" has become a synonym for disaster, but Moody gives this tension an historical dimension in the centerpiece of the collection, a retelling of the Lewis and Clark expedition structured around the weather that threatened, and ultimately determined it: in one poem, he states "weather / we want // to control"; in another, he observes "weather won't / leave, no matter / our attention to / it."

But ultimately, it is not his content that directs the climate of this book; it is his mastery of the elements of language. Just listen:

> Land absorbs sound, deflects some. Traffic tries too
> hard, neglecting sun's sheets, meaning grief. I'd say
> belief is altogether wrong, but I'd be alone—for one,
> ground soon becomes softer than first thought, less
> than seconds after.

He will go on in the next line to rhyme that "after" with "disaster," in an instance of his continual, delicate application of his theme. But it's above all sound that's leading here, and it's sound that fosters intricate and telling connections, such as that among "sheets," "grief," and "belief," all orbiting obliquely around the first syllable of "meaning." Other links hold "sun," "wrong," "alone," and "one" together in a constellation created by tight sequences that create a commentary that both runs parallel to and deviates from the trajectory of the whole.

Though ostensibly prose, the tight interweave of sound binds the text into a single, seamless gesture that is distinctly poetic in its ability to disrupt linguistic clarity, that supposedly ideal one-to-one relationship between sign and referent, in ways that offer additional relationships, and thus additional dimensions of sensation and possibility. It's these tangled threads of potential that Moody chases through his acute attention. And this attention is always focused on the actual, the incidental, the mundane.

His relentless interest in the weather is, in part, a way of insisting upon the integrity of the daily, and just as he constructs constellations of sounds, he also creates constellations of the common objects of the world (tree, statue, grass, house, fog), letting them become, on the one hand, emblems of both the specific and the generic, and on the other, recurring occasions for flights of speculation, in which chains of association lead him forth.

His is a weather that works both inside and out, and neither is metaphoric—that would be too easy, and he is always careful not to fall into that, but instead to adhere as closely as possible to a base of lived experience, to an experience of the elements, and a deep appreciation of the aesthetic engagement that each day's weather offers us. Its dynamics, its rhythms, its scents, sights, and sounds are absolutely unique, and they assail each one of our senses, bringing them all together in a constant synesthetic event.

But the elements are not always dramatic, and despite its headlines and their hyperbole, the weather is actually often all but invisible. It's the background; we live in it without living it, and it is this level of weather in which Moody is perhaps most deeply invested. The fact that wind is invisible, that rain has no color, that light and snow are both clear white—here in these apparent transparencies, Moody finds the subtleties that actually shape our lives.

"[T]o write is to die / into," he writes—into the elements, into Lewis' ice—"*I . . . wrote untill verry late / at night. . . .*"

Cole Swensen

1

We Use Spoons Mostly

What this says
about a human, as opposed to, say,
another beast, has everything to do
with electricity and warmth. Through the window

to the backyard, the river crystal-clear
like glass. Like glass? Is it human
to be redundant and to overstate
the obvious? The river, crystal-clear

between the floorboards, under
my feet, and under your feet, and the way we stand may
or may not alter its course. When was our last
rain, wasn't it Saturday, I'm pretty sure?

What memory performs as opposed to,
say, the sounds outside this window. There are
birds, and there are cicadas. There
are cicadas and there are birds and even crickets—

Hello, this moment has just recently passed.
We close our eyes more often than we think.
Let me just say, again and very quickly, one
last time, Hello.

What We First Said

The tiniest oak tree
                    in the tiniest room—
as we feel our eyes, our greedy joints
unhinge and root.

(The body floats, like a red sail of surveillance.)

            In the history of human suffering
this must be what we meant:
                    an eye or an ear,
replaced with hard clay, or a plum.

Climate Reply

Weather as if to repeat. Weather to read a name.
As if to ask a question, weather to strip the mane,

to feed the cats, to sleep. Go inside, weather to weep, split the maw.

Plant the plants, weather to eat the dead, their roots as if to speak.

Weather to number the names, hold the sheets
over bodies, blind as blue.   Weather as if to flame.

Scrape the storm of its howl. Cellar as if to swarm, night as if to rot.

Ground warm with flesh, ears as if to watch. Cover the eyes
with weather, weigh them down with skin.

The dead's steady hum, weather as if to win.

A Weather

Why a. Why not bring bodies back to home. Bones before our tracks, after parks cleared leaves. Why radio. Listen listlessly, then sleep. Why weather becomes a lack—language suffers, like you. Paths, too, refuse use. Why department. Why soda. Five calendars of blue. Light lingers long as memory, but why winter. Music wanes, despite the view.

The Fallacy of Perfection

I'm sitting in a chair in the middle of a field,
barely visible through cold fog.
A tattered notebook and a glass of water
lay on the grass, near my feet.
Who knows how I got here.
I decide to write about the fog,
which is fog, which is cold, which is
concealing, which—suddenly—
is the one-eyed rabbit I've seen before,
running from under a pine.
Was it looking for food? Or is it now?
Or does this even matter?
Back to the fog, which is fog,
which is isolating, which—again, suddenly—
is a bird from a friend's backyard:
a blue jay, curiously alone.

I won't lie to you. It is difficult,
keeping these projections to myself.
I take a sip of water. The grass,
in this fog, is it still green? These words
cannot be helped; they are—and are not—
soaked with reality. Save yourself
while you can. The fog is growing thicker.

A Weather

Snow falls thick like waxed shards of paper, white collecting
flat over ground. Now reconsider walking. Trees don't mind,
limbs no resistance, waiting to react till spring. Indoors,
windows are erasures, at best. Worse, when shades are kept
drawn, the world—purely physical: touch the desk, touch
the counter, sink inside myself for lack of observation.
Hummingbirds won't happen. Neither will melt nor peel
nor scar. Waiting to bite, I palm a cold grape—the hand
asks difficult questions.

Like Hearing For from That

THAT COLOR SHOULD BE GIVEN CHOICE

Breathing,
I ache something
frost. That runners should molt
hate away. Sunshine quilts older
homes brown.

•

FROM A PATIO

Weather
brings a scraping:
animal this, skin swells
shoulders, shoulders. Moreover, I
sand brooms.

•

FOR OPPEN

Black oak
settles—leaves, then
dust, my mouth shaped around
grappling. That lunchbox filled, spilling
new lawns.

•

HEARING WHAT IS HEARD

Owl sounds
dry a field. Quick,
perception's drip, monster
my mind. Niedecker whispers time's
trickle.

•

LIKE A WINDOW LOOKS

Winter:
no room—cold grass
closed a market, soon to
appreciate air. Bare words bear
these trees.

Chatter

There was once a glacier
here. Now it has become
Nebraska. Which was

"flat water." Which tells
something of time
thus something

of death. If we live
believing the sky meets
ground, somewhere—

where are we talking?
More importantly, we are still
talking about Nebraska.

A Weather

Land absorbs sound, deflects some. Traffic tries too hard, neglecting sun's sheets, meaning grief. I'd say belief is altogether wrong, but I'd be alone—for one, ground soon becomes softer than first thought, less than seconds after. I relive each disaster the same: plot disrupts a moment earned, allowing time to reconvene. When I'm looking through a window I'm also looking through a screen.

This Forest Isn't a Room

The trees are always laughing down on you.
They bare their branches—you stare at your legs.

The trees and you are different—they have water, continually consume.
They have trunks wider than your body.

Their trunks don't shake when they laugh, you notice.
You cannot remember what your body does

but you believe your body's not a tree, a tree not a body.
Shake with cold like you shake with cold.

The trees,
they shake their leaves like walls in the wind.

A Feather Protruding from the Mouth

Weather, for the moment, behind windows.
Curtains intensely made of red. This was why
we couldn't see behind them, and this was why
we didn't want to.

Light around the room fluttered with light—
wax dripped like filmed caverns.
I could still see your hand, which, for all I knew,
could've exploded any second.

Through the wall, our "hand" might've been "land,"
"sand," or "band." But it was all of these.
At the same moment you sneezed, a bird,
or something else with feathers, flew through the doorway.

Of course we didn't see it
so our "flew" could've been "blue," "glue," or "God."

A Weather

While waiting, weather brings its storm—rain again,
past trees, these instances to pause. But last night the TV
said "bright." Buying back such a hint, inside becomes
evocative: framed paintings offer more doors, lesser pleas.
Tomorrow, crows announce pallid company. Winter,
without smell, leaves.

The Seating

Blue chair on its plastic back. Grass
and its green leaning
                        toward the dirt. More
is what we've wanted, and now—
a cue from the trees: consider the security
of your silences. Forget.
            Listen when the earth becomes self-aware
and take the red chair in your hand, set it
on the ground; sit down.

A Weather

Said sand molds shape, said a statue is a marker of time—
that crop, once plowed, heeds product, was worked till
work waned to sleep. Before, over mealtime meat we spoke
to soothe future uses, shallow calls. Which was all we knew
to do: swollen promise, eager ear, new duties unfolding like
each new year.

Salina, Kansas

This flatness is a sickness.
But this sickness can be cured
with a house.

So for Susan
he built one. Till his hands were tired
he built one, then added

on, etcetera.
"As much as the sky
swallows the landscape,"

he'd say, "this
is how much I love you."
He'd say this

but he wouldn't
mean it. He'd have one
hand covering his eyes.

Susan knew. She'd leave
the hot sky for her cool
floor. On the linoleum

she'd wonder, "Is this
how God terrifies? Or is this
just the horizon?"

Outside the house, all over
the yard, their children lay looking
like desperate actors.

A Weather

Summer's scalding echo—sediment left when water recedes, waves creating distance. A blanket draped on a tree, once grass. I'm taken by good manners, as god-awful awnings become dust, but talk of texture is beyond us. A simple sentence might reflect simplicity. Converse could be true, too. The flower will bend from its vase before breaking. Without liquid, dryness carves out incarnate lungs.

Dear Ghosts,

1. APPLES IN THE HOUSE

In the middle of the night, when the fruit
is scariest. I hold my hand out

and I feel your nibbling. Don't worry,
my eyes are still closed. I've only

peeked that once. The cold
that is your breath—these windows

of fog. If I were outside
I'd read your backward name again and again.

2. TAKING A BATH IN GRAVY

Shh. Just listen—
our two bodies, coated.

If I said brown, I'd be doing
a disservice. We both

know that. I'd feed you
by the spoonful, but such

ridiculousness, to think
of a spoon! So just tell me

like you do when I dream.
This time, don't scream.

3. PINECONES ON THE COFFEE TABLE

And this won't do. One on the stove,
one under my bed sheets. You know

this just won't work. If cinnamon
smells like the hands of a baby

then, by nightfall, I don't want
to smell anything that's alive.

4. HUM OF THE FRIDGE LIKE THOUGHT

No matter the temperature—
the banana cut in half

always turns brown. Add this
to the list. When I open the fridge

in the middle of the night, I can hear
you thinking behind me.

5. IN THE BEGINNING THERE WERE LEFTOVERS

All this is to say, you still
surprise me. But it's more like fear

when it's dark. Your breath,
suddenly, on my face

then your two big eyes!—
So at first, I would stay up and eat

but the night was always calling me in.

6. LIKE DUST AROUND THE LIGHT FIXTURE

So the morning came. The light bulb
didn't matter. I unscrewed it,

something as warm as flesh,
and put it in my pocket.

So you see, the days
were manageable. That is, the days

were when I missed you the most.

7. MORE THAN DOORS

Have we become too
one-sided? Knock once if you believe

in structural security, twice
for mutual relationships. If I don't hear

a knock, I'll assume you're reserving
judgment, since beauty is both

conditional, subjective. Then again if I hear

nothing, my throat might well up so that
I can't speak clearly. Breathe even.

8. THIS TIME, THE FRESH PAINT

What'd I tell you? Keep your hands off
the walls. Just remember when

I say this, I mean *please*.

9. SO TO SAY THE SKY

has left us both behind,
if I were to say, would mean

by now we share something
in common. Two footprints

in the dust. A flashlight
wanes. You know what I mean.

Both—"Your face!" and "That's not
your face." Either way, what comforts me

most is how my heart
still beats, and how somewhere

something is listening.

10. SAM COOKE ON THE RADIO, ALONE

That's funny. But I've never heard that song
before. What a thing to do, to think

about love as something real.
When I think about you

it reminds me of the time I sang
so loud my throat bled.

2

Lancaster County Notebook

The Good Life

the Small Pox reduced the others
—William Clark, 10 March 1805

How to begin

How to write
about a place
uninhabited

*those Chiefs Stayed all day
and all night*

Beal Slough we see
bridged
by highway

A moment

Do salt flats a city
make

*gave us man[y]
Strang accounts of his nation &c*

A city

How to write about a place

*five Villages
on the West Side & two on the East*

What do we
know
we know

And how do we know
to begin

Travelogue

—John Ordway, 14 March 1805

Those *who we expected*
would go with us
are gone, leaving
us alone

to pray into silence.
The physical world
we once
knew

also is gone—it
has taken *another notion*
and has pitched
a lodge

outside of the Garrison
and moved out. When winter
wind begins
to warm

and geese are seen
flying north, there is something
there that *has joined*
in his place.

To, But

a Frenchman who has lived many years with the Ricares & Mandans
shewed us the process used by those Indians to make beads
   —Meriwether Lewis, 16 March 1805

A siren
alerts us
to what

we can't see,
weather
we want

to control, but
the art
is kept a secret

into which we've
no entry
but need

to believe
is yet known
to but few

of them who
soon
will show us.

Attention

—William Clark, 25 March 1805

The ice began
to brake away
this evening—
from indoors
where sound
reminds us—
weather won't
leave, no matter
our attention to
it—*near distroying*
our Canoes as they
wer decnding to the fort.

In Crossing

but few Indians visit us to day [. . .] those people are fond of those
animals ta[i]nted and Catch great numbers every Spring
    —William Clark, 28 March 1805

These jobs for
which we wake,
these reasons

to spend in
the warming air—
incentive

to make what one
can make—collect
what's worth collecting—

they are watching
to catch the floating
Buffalow which brake

through the ice in Crossing—
what I discard
and what I hold

onto, an act not
of need but an act
similar to faith

By Hand

—William Clark, 2 April 1805

Missing the moon
last night, I tried
to make myself see
something more:
to write is to die
into. *I conclude*
to Send my journal
to the President far away—
wrote untill verry late
at night but little time
to devote to my friends.

Act of Interpretation

we Sent an interpreter to See with orders to return imediately and let
us know if their Chiefs ment to go down to See their great father
   —William Clark, 6 April 1805

Wanting
to witness

where I'm
not: a problem

of location
but *all the birds*

that we believe
visit this country

have now returned.
As to see

is to believe
to believe is

not to see, as *we*
are informed of

the arrival
of the ricarra nation

on the other Side
of the river near

their old village.

Only What

the beautifull eagle, or calumet bird, *so called from the circumstance*
of the natives decorating their pipe-stems with it's plumage
 —Meriwether Lewis and William Clark, 8 April 1805

To say only
what I can
say is not

an admission
of faith
but guilt:

the only birds
that I obseved
during the winter:

a catalog to
control the
body's limit

Spring

—John Ordway, 9 April 1805

When winter
has gone for good
we're left with
more than thought
yet not ready to feel
when *the Musquetoes*
begin to Suck our blood
this afternoon

Between Both

—Meriwether Lewis, 15 April 1805

I walked on shore, somewhere
I had never been,
to locate a river, a tree,
a place I never knew

I wanted, *it being*
an invariable rule
between observer
and observed

not to be both absent
for fear of what
I hoped to know
at the same time

Nourishment

—William Clark, 15 April 1805

Rain ruins ground's
footing, forcing
us to eat inside.

Frozen, fried
fish nuggets
for the oven,

TV's hum warming
the plate, the fork—
a large Strong pen

made for Catching
the antelope—
enters the mouth

where we locate
pleasure, once
sustenance, that

feeds us—*with wings*
projecting from it
widining from the pen.

Distance

I think the quantity of timbered land on the river is increasing
    —Meriwether Lewis, 16 April 1805

Sun erases yesterday's
news I now
can see completely—

the hills of the river still
continue extreemly broken—

but how long until one
no longer can see—

when it becomes a fine
level country of open fertile lands—

the history of handling
the inaccessible—

the mineral appearances
still continue—

and still I think
that somehow this
is all I can know

An Explanation

the Indian account of them dose not corrispond with our experience so far
— Meriwether Lewis, 17 April 1805

Cold again
yet *we saw immence*
quantities of game
in every direction.

Visible versus
invisible, writing past
into present *tho' we*
continue to see

many tracks of the bear
we have seen
but very few of them
which we know

exist among us
and those are at a great
distance generally runing
from us; I thefore

presume that they are
extreemly wary and shy
as if reason alone
explains appearance.

That Abstraction

—Meriwether Lewis, 18 April 1805

one Beaver caught
this morning
by two traps,
having a foot
in each

as weather warms
it brings
us outside,
never quite
warm enough

the traps belonged
to different
individuals, between
whom, a contest
ensued

how to settle
weather, determine
that abstract mass:
private property,
the cold

which would have
terminated
had not our timely
arrival
prevented it

Perfect Potential

saw several parsels of buffaloe's hair hanging on the rose bushes,
which had been bleached by exposure to the weather and became
perfectly white
    —Meriwether Lewis, 18 April 1805

appearance of the wool
of the sheep, tho' much finer
and more silkey and soft

material to clothe,
to house, to protect
from the unknowable

though knowledge
lacks correlation
with conviction

I am confident
that an excellent cloth
may be made

of the wool
of the Buffaloe
and I am confident

that we will never
not attempt to make
up for any lack

3

Same-Day Resolution

Since the time spring
has been here, I've
allowed myself two things:
clouds filled with weather
and skies filled

with clouds. As each
offers a separate perspective
my brain's consoled only
on both sides. The train
that passes through town

barely stops. But because
of it, money is money and time
time. Funny, the way
decision dictates so much—
I'm hungry, generally,

consistently, at a quarter
past three, though
my stomach's filled
so slow I often forget
when I've forgotten to eat.

A Weather

Since it is raining, and it is something, why can't we all agree to have fun with weather's nothing? Sooner than showers can clean us of scars, certain words travel only so far— Texas, alone, doesn't tell me too much, but stripped of its T a meaning erupts. As in: Where do babies come from? As in: The phrase by itself. As wind predicts an economy, it's when either one lapses that either is felt.

Both

A new moon
blooms
from behind
low-lying clouds.

River's water
that I only
heard
now glistens.

Barn owl
of my childhood
both here
and not here.

Everything Is Not for Everyone

Wind works
the whining
house—

a reminder
of accessibility.
Two clocks

in one room
don't make anything
easier.

I'm not writing
this because
I have to.

My mind occupies
through a window
a few

separate things.

A Weather

A certain sound decays ground: a final call for all the walking. What is it with this weather that we can't stop talking? Humid-hot, I won't be waiting long. Last time surrounded with folks' sporadic yawns I couldn't sleep. But that's another story, another lawn that isn't really greener when you're in it neck-deep. Even camping inside a car—mosquitoes, like us, are never too far from water.

Yes, This Is May

Rain blurs
the window—cattle,
distant, huddle
near the fence line.

From someone's
notebook: "clouds
bring with them
other life."

Though this
weather muddles
the mountaintop,
sun still

warms the field's
wet center. Wind
I hear
moos for a moment.

A Weather

Heat: winter's memory, a blast rushed past. Walking over streets impedes touch—attempts to border order, once lost. Raking long-dead leaves removes most, but causes dust. Summer shower drained into a ditch: collected at a later date, water creates nourishment. Oil altogether different in use, suffused everywhere, only spread to some. Oklahoma, arid land demands more fun.

Exercise in Patience

He watches waves
repeat themselves. Far away
on a mountain, a rock
moves, uncovering
a cave—but nothing

enters, nothing exits.
"I'm okay with this,"
he thinks. But it is difficult
to determine whether
he is thinking

about the cave or about
the ceaseless waves.
Just as I was writing
this I heard a bird
hit the window, which

I didn't realize till
it was flying, perfectly,
away. The man still waits
there, on the beach, for
I don't know what.

Backyard

I am here. So far
this seems to have been true.

•

Tainted
by summer's
decay, darker

thoughts
carved into
tree bark

dampen.

•

Leaves flutter
on an October branch.
I shouldn't compare
this to laughter.

•

Focus fixed on a silver maple.
          Suddenly in
my sight line, the mind:
a pine needle hangs
from a spiderweb's strand.

•

Crickets consume daylight
with their song—or is it
that their song

emits darkness? That either
isn't feasible
frightens me.

•

The backyard dims.
Similar
to those moments
before sleep.

•

Morning glory opens to
new sun—rather
same sun
            becomes
perceivable.

•

Pin oak left
me with its leaves, each
a somewhat familiar word.

•

Fence posts pock
a border; sun
fades south-facing
siding. Nowhere
          exists
stability.

•

Leafless tree—
I can't say anything
without projecting
my need for warmth.

•

Crickets sing sooner
each evening. Are they terrified
like I am?

•

Moonlight: I can barely see
my hand.

.

Ryegrass wet
from morning—
filled with night
a nearby child cries.

.

Sitting in a chair
I'm full of absurdities.
Wind blows—

I can't make sense
of it, even.

.

I hear, above me—
no, I see
geese flying
south. So these
words say.

•

The mailman cracks the mailbox
closed. He must be smiling
a little too hard
for a Tuesday.

A Weather

Colors claim consistency but, with time's trained removal, change: red becomes a dusk-soaked meadow, while on a hill orange is a lantern-lit tent. How parchment settles this debt, I'm unsure, at best. Sky stays only so far away, though a hand never will not touch, no matter. Two days without rain—a row of corn that could be meat, could be fatter, as hereafter profits dictate what will be known as need.

A Note on Silence

Atop a hill sits a house,
abandoned, made of trees
similar to those
surrounding it. A lone coyote
howls at the doorstep

smelling prey. This
goes on for months; the door
never opens. Leaves begin to fall
on the coyote, growing

thinner every day. Soon
all the leaves have been stripped
from their trees—as the coyote
deserts the house, each move
can be heard for miles. Now

alone, the door opens; wind
clears the hilltop of leaves. Somewhere
a crying woman lights a candle
to warm her hands.

This Hemisphere of Leaves

The moon kept finding
me through the trees, or I found
the moon between objects—
both were probably true.

I was nervous. You could see
this in my walk.
In such a quiet hemisphere, my steps
were tiny disturbances.

I am not the moon, nor am I the tree.
What is writing. What is debris.

A Weather

Cold covers everything, numbs thumbs. A sequence made of stillness: bitter wishes, better watches, buttered waffles, battered Walmarts. Not to say which month is superior—stitching gaps cracked with silence. At best an advertisement, to write this requires sound that seeps from slippage.

Praise

Bless the tree, for without it
to what could we compare ourselves?
Bless its sturdy trunk, which keeps it strong,
rooted in the unseen, a balance
we know doubly. Bless its branches,
where snow builds thin homes in winter,
where spring brings perfumed promise,
where summer presents—as Ponge says—
"their verbiage, a flood, a vomit of green."
Bless these arms, like our arms,
that cannot catch anything,
that can only absorb coincidence,
that—without their hands—lack economy.
Bless the wind and the dirt and the rain
that travel around—and sometimes into—
these arms, desperate as they are
to hold. In fall, bless the tree's tiny deaths,
each one of them, as they collect
on our sleeves and crumble under our feet.
In these ends we understand simile;
somehow we create consolation.
Bless the snow that soon will cover
all this verbiage.

A Weather

Complex countertops feed heat: reflect touch's talk, which hearkens back to stop. Sunday morning and coffee pot. Tuesday evening but elastic. Information's information, we see so clearly. Two ducks drink water, wait, float. Wind listens, though I lack insight. If we make midnight, if we make mudslide, if we spell winter with a y. One day, my teeth will freeze from time, however hummingbirds interpret ten.

Remembering the Original

I saw the man standing in the field at dawn.
        He stood like a small storm.
I looked at the sky and saw the fields coming.
Waves.   The tiny storms were on their way.

Dear—

I said Ghost because I couldn't
say anything better. I said
I'd wait a while but I

was clearly wrong. If convenience
mattered most, I would've eaten my fruit
in silence, but I said Fast

as if I had a choice. Then
I said Sleep with my childhood voice.
Dreams came, or they

were already there. So I said Sickness
which was what I meant. I'd say
I was accurate but only

in attempt. I thought
and I thought. I said Ghost because,
once, I could not.

Notes and Acknowledgments

This book's title comes from R. W. Franklin's *The Poems of Emily Dickinson* (Harvard University Press), poem 1269, whose first quatrain reads:

> I thought that nature was enough
> Till Human nature came
> But that the other did absorb
> As Parallax a Flame –

"The Seating" is after Katherine Fraser's *The Director*, printed in *New American Paintings* No. 63 (The Open Studios Press).

The italicized language in the second section is taken from *The Lewis and Clark Journals*, edited by Gary E. Moulton (University of Nebraska Press).

The quote in "Praise" is from C. K. Williams's translation of Francis Ponge's "The Cycle of Seasons," from his *Selected Poems* (Wake Forest University Press).

These poems were written in Alpine, El Dorado, Lancaster, and Travis Counties.

•

Thanks to the editors of the following magazines and anthologies for first publishing many of these poems: *American Letters & Commentary*, *Anti-*, *Best New Poets 2009* (University of Virginia Press), *Bigger Than They Appear: Anthology of Very Short Poems* (Accents Publishing), *Boston Review*, *Denver Quarterly*, *DIAGRAM*, *DIAGRAM.4* (New Michigan Press), *Indiana Review*, *Linebreak*, *Little Red Leaves*, *OmniVerse*, *past simple*, *Quarterly West*, *Route 7 Review*, *SHAMPOO*, *Sixth Finch*, *Washington Square*, and *Witness*. Some of these poems were published in the chapbooks *Climate Reply* (New Michigan Press) and *Once Was a Weather* (Greying Ghost Press).

Special thanks to Jeff Alessandrelli, Carl Annarummo, Grace Bauer, Steve Behrendt, John Chávez, Nick Courtright, Sarah Gorham, Fran Kaye, Ander Monson, Kathleen Peirce, James Shea, Bret Shepard, Cole Swensen, Joshua Ware, Steve Wilson, and my family.

TREY MOODY was born and raised in San Antonio, Texas. He holds an MFA in Creative Writing from Texas State University and a PhD in English from the University of Nebraska–Lincoln. *Thought That Nature* is his first book.